HERMAN MILLER
1939 CATALOG
GILBERT ROHDE
MODERN DESIGN

HERMAN MILLER
1939 CATALOG
GILBERT ROHDE
MODERN DESIGN

PREFACE BY: LESLIE PIÑA

WITH VALUE GUIDE

Schiffer Publishing Ltd

4880 Lower Valley Rd. Atglen, PA 19310 USA

Front matter layout by Bonnie Hensley
Geometr231 Bt Bold/Geometr415 Lt Bt

ISBN: 0-7643-0501-8
Printed in the United States of America

Published by Schiffer Publishing Ltd.
4880 Lower Valley Road
Atglen, PA 19310
Phone: (610) 593-1777; Fax: (610) 593-2002
E-mail: Schifferbk@aol.com
Please write for a free catalog.
This book may be purchased from the publisher.
Please include $3.95 for shipping.

Please try your bookstore first.

We are interested in hearing from authors
with book ideas on related subjects.

Preface

In 1927, while the Herman Miller Furniture Company was content to manufacture historic reproduction bedroom suites, American designer Gilbert Rohde visited Europe. There he saw two extremes in modern furnishings — the traditionally handcrafted pieces made of exotic materials and those of tubular metal suited for mass production. Both versions of the style (later called Art Deco) were found in France and Germany, though today the French are noted for their use of extravagant wood veneers and inlay, while the Germans, especially those affiliated with the Bauhaus, are known for austere designs using mundane materials like bent metal tubes.

In 1930, Herman Miller was feeling the weight of the Depression. As the story goes, according to *Business as Unusual*, the book by former company head Hugh De Pree, on a hot day in July in 1930, when a man walked into the Grand Rapids showroom and introduced himself as Gilbert Rohde, D.J. De Pree (Hugh's father) listened. Rohde offered De Pree a philosophy of design and a way to transform the business. His bold ideas seemed less risky to a company with a glum economic outlook and with little to lose. Rohde's furniture designs were clearly influenced by the French Art Deco and German modernism he had found so compelling during his recent travels. A third, and the most critical ingredient of Rohde's design solution, was the concept of industrialization. Industrial design was then a fledgling field practiced by a small but elite group of American designers equipped with backgrounds in graphic art rather than engineering. It was enjoying its debut complete with (printed) media coverage in the late 1920s and early 1930s, and Rohde was one of its prominent proponents. Rohde's interpretive styling and innovative use of modern materials, manufacturing techniques, and modular forms would convert Herman Miller from being a follower of European historicism into a leader of American modernism. Mass production and mass marketing were about to save Herman Miller's bottom line.

When De Pree saw Rohde's first drawings, he thought they looked like something from a manual training school, and he told him. Rohde replied in a letter by explaining the advantages of simplicity. Without surface enrichment, carvings, or moldings to cover joints and potentially imperfect construction, there was a clear need for precision. Designing toward structural integrity and precise joinery was intended to replace mere decoration. He also wrote that furniture should be anonymous, because people are more important than the furniture. It should be useful and planned for the people living in the rooms. Therefore, furniture should be space saving, utilitarian, and multipurpose. These ideas led to one of Rohde's most significant contributions — the use of modular, or sectional, seating and cabinetry in which interchangeability and flexibility is integral to the design. His were the shoulders on which successor George Nelson would later stand.

It was a new direction for the Herman Miller Furniture Company and for the consumer. According to De Pree, Rohde elevated the company's thinking from selling merely furniture to selling a way of life. By 1932 Rohde was designing all of Herman Miller's modern furniture, and the 1933 catalog introduced the first modern lines, including those for the famous "Designed for Living" House at the 1933 Chicago World's Fair. By January 1935, Rohde already had suggested that Herman Miller focus on modern design, even if it meant dropping the traditional line. In 1936 a major decision was made to discontinue period furniture and manufacture only high quality modern furniture. De Pree felt that there was a kind of dishonesty in copying old pieces and faking finishes to get an Old World antique look. The country was at the threshold of an era of new materials, tools, and techniques. The time was ripe for modern furniture.

Until traditional furniture was entirely phased out (it was still included in the 1940 catalog and would not totally disappear until Rohde's death in 1944) it was made in the same factory along with modern. Herman Miller realized soon after its introduction that modern design gave them more furniture for their dollar, that good modern design would be longer lived, and that over time it would be more economical to produce. Even so, the decision was made in a marketing climate of apathetic stores and a lack of vision among most industry contemporaries. Herman Miller needed to go directly to the people who were ready to live with modern design — hence, the showroom. Rohde designed the showrooms — Grand Rapids in 1935, Chicago in 1938, and New York in 1941. Beginning in 1933, Herman Miller was the first American furniture manufacturer to focus on modern design, and by 1945 they produced nothing but. The New York showroom was the first of its kind devoted exclusively to modern furniture. Gilbert Rohde was the force behind this great beginning.

This 1939 Product and Sales Catalog is an historical document. It not only illustrates the modern (and traditional) designs from 1939, it includes lines from previous years. They are easily identified, because according to the company's early numbering system, the first two digits of most model numbers indicate the year of introduction. Since this catalog includes some of Rohde's earliest (1933) Herman Miller items, a sense of the evolution of his designs and of American modernism through the 1930s can be gained. Also shown are a few examples of Rohde's extraordinary clocks, made by the Herman Miller Clock Company (later the Howard Miller Clock Company).

The exotic woods shown in this catalog — East India Rosewood, Brazilian Rosewood, Sequoia Burl, Walnut Burl, Mardou Burl, Quilted Maple, Macassar Ebony — are reminiscent of the opulence of French Art Deco. Clean lines and combinations of contrasting light and dark woods — Paldao with Quilted Maple, Walnut with Bleached Maple, White Acer with Black Walnut — exemplify American as well as European Art Deco styling. Some of Rohde's chrome plated tubular steel models were inspired by French designs; others were innovative and original. Tubular steel furniture, though introduced in Europe in the mid-1920s, was new and exciting in America in the early '30s, and

Herman Miller became one of its leading manufacturers. His use of bentwood for chair frames and drum-shaped cabinets show both European design inspiration and the foundation for later forms. The biomorphic shaped table tops, often associated with post World War II design, were actually Rohde innovations of the '30s. And his use of plastics is equally forward looking. The lucite table legs and tops and the plexiglass drawer and door pulls were early, innovative, high style applications of these plastics. In addition to the outstanding, varied, and sometimes pioneering design represented in the following pages, imaginative use of modern materials also fills the pages of this important company catalog. Clearly, both the designer and manufacturer of these classic examples of modern furniture have made a substantial contribution to the evolution of American modernism.

Leslie Piña, Ph.D.
October 1997

Accounts of Rohde's philosophy are from *Business as Unusual*. Catalog and cover photographs are courtesy of Herman Miller, Inc.

1939 Catalog and Sales Guide

THE HERMAN MILLER FURNITURE COMPANY
ZEELAND, MICHIGAN

"I do not know any reading more easy, more fascinating, more delightful than a catalogue.

All the historical books which contain no lies are extremely tedious."

ANATOLE FRANCE

Galleries of American Design

Modern and Traditional

INFORMATION FOR THE SALESPERSONS

●

This book is in two sections: Modern beginning on page 4; Traditional beginning on page 62.

The Modern is arranged somewhat in the order which would be followed in planning a home. Beginning with the living room make a list of the utilities desired. Then plan the available wall space; next the important seating; and after that the tables and occasional pieces.

The first Wall Unit Section with tables and multi-purpose pieces to match illustrates the Laurel group, page 4 to 13.

Second — A Mahogany group; page 14 to 18.

Third — A Walnut group; page 19 to 27.

Then follows combination chairs, sofas, lounging chairs, occasional chairs, and chairs for bedroom and dining room.

Next the formal dining rooms, and finally the bedrooms.

The Traditional groups begin on page 62.

"QUALITY" *talks.*

The making of furniture is a maze of detail. An average dresser requires 332 operations to complete. 272 of these are done by machinery. Yet these 272 machine operations represent less than 35% of the total labor hours, and about 65% of the time allowance is taken by the 60 hand operations. Even in a so-called mass production plant this ratio is practically the same. The price paid for furniture is therefore largely determined by the amount of handwork and the quality of materials used. A few examples of these in Herman Miller furniture are listed here.

Only high grade cabinet woods used.

Selection and matching of fine veneers.

Our curved veneer parts are usually made of eleven plys laid in forms which assures more permanency and uniformity than four plys on a band-sawed core, which is the common way of doing it.

Flush effects which are an important requisite in pure modern design, are the result of precision machining and careful fitting of long mitres; and these are both impossible without trained men and good equipment.

Handwork still is the only way to properly produce many of the quality earmarks in a piece, such as: fitting drawers and corner blocks; preparation of wood for finishing; padding; toning; glazing; distressing; antiquing; and block rubbing the final finish.

See paragraph on upholstering for other hidden qualities in Herman Miller furniture.

FINISHES:

The standard finish for each wood in the group is mentioned. Special finishes can be obtained at approximately 10% extra. Different woods can usually be finished in matching colors, although grain effects cannot be made to match.

Pieces are only finished as orders are received. This insures factory fresh pieces. Time required for this is usually ten days unless pieces are temporarily out of stock, in which case you will be promptly notified.

Wood samples of finishes in which you are interested can be mailed promptly on request.

ABOUT THE FINISH:

The efforts of many "hand workmen" combine to produce the Herman Miller finish. From white stock to the final satin glow of the rubbed finish the trained hands of expert finishers add their bit to the built-up finish applied to all Miller furniture.

Color-fast penetrating stains give the depth so necessary to really fine pieces; carefully applied washcoats protect the cleanliness of the fine veneers while numerous hand sandings prepare the surfaces for their protective coats. Filling is hand-wiped to smooth every pore and then thoroughly dried. Further sizing with the all important hand sand prepares for skillful glazing, padding, toning and shading, to bring out the true richness of the woods.

To protect this acquired beauty multiple coats of the finest lacquers are used. Hard drying sealers are applied as a foundation coating with special attention being given to elasticity and check prevention. These pyroxylin coatings have been tested for durability. Sealers are again hand sanded before the application of the first lacquer coating. After the first coat of lacquer has been applied it is thoroughly dried and "nub-sanded" before the second coat is applied. The final coat is thoroughly dried to carefully prepared schedules to insure no shrinkage or blooming of final finish. The backs, drawers, and interior parts are given protective lacquer coats to seal out unwanted moisture and the piece moves on to hand rubbers and polishers.

In the rubbing department the full beauty of the piece comes to light with fine pumice and rubbing oil — **a felt block** — and the **clever hands** of **selected** men. The trained sense of touch developed by these men allows them to literally smooth the top coats to velvet sheens — not removing too much nor too little — of the protecting coats, but only that which is necessary to produce the satin smoothness of the truly built-up finish. Miller furniture is COMPLETELY hand-rubbed—not just tops nor fronts nor selected first glance areas. Miller furniture is FINISHED ALL OVER with equal attention, to give lasting beauty and enduring satisfaction to the purchaser. A liberal coating of hard wax which is applied by hand completes the finest finish which can be applied to wood — a finish which fascinates — a finish which contains glamour, a glamour which excites admiration.

UPHOLSTERY CONSTRUCTION:

The deep seated chairs and sofas are made in only one high grade seven point construction:

1. Full close-webbed bottom, held to frames by long shank nails (not tacks).

2. Individual tempered steel springs, sewed to webbing four times.

3. Eight no-slip knot tied with Italian twine, and frame edges rounded to avoid cutting twine.

4. All horse hair filling under long staple white cotton.

5. All easy chairs with tight seats double-springed and double-stuffed, to give the maximum comfort of loose cushions and the tailored effect of tight seats.

6. Muslin cover under fabric making a double cover.

7. Only double-dowelled, sound hardwood frames are used: reinforced with substantial hand-fitted corner blocks glued and screwed.

UPHOLSTERY FABRICS:

A wide selection of upholstery fabrics in nine grades and a variety of colors is available. When requesting sample swatches, be sure to state customer's color preference. Muslin prices include the covering of the piece with your fabric if you wish to send in your own cover.

Upholstery is done on a custom basis; that is, the frames are carried in stock and upholstered to order. Therefore, orders for upholstered pieces are not subject to cancellation.

INTERIOR DESIGN SERVICE:

If you desire suggestions as to room arrangements, colors, and accessories, please send a rough floor plan giving important dimensions, the placement of windows, doors, and radiators, and state any special utilities that are desired in the room.

HOW TO JUDGE MODERN DESIGN

The acceptance and the permanence of Modern design is no longer questioned. The question is now changed to "What Modern is good and what is bad?" "How can the consumer tell?"

He can judge in the same manner in which he has judged furniture in the past — by the name of the designer and maker. Sheraton furniture is good because Sheraton was a good designer; so with Chippendale and Hepplewhite.

For nearly a hundred years the designer was forgotten. There is no important name since Duncan Phyfe, until the advent of the modern idea.

Today the modern school of design is as solidly grounded in contemporary culture as any that has gone before. There is nothing superficial about it. It is as firmly rooted in the necessities of our economic and social state, our way of living, as was the idea of the Elizabethan craftsmen or those of the Eighteenth Century.

Foremost in this school stands Gilbert Rohde. His contribution has received recognition the world over.

The Herman Miller Furniture Company was among the first to sponsor "designer designed" modern furniture at a time when everyone said modern was dead forever. Every piece of Herman Miller Modern is an original Rohde design, and is imbued with the spirit of this country's foremost modernist.

THE GROUPING IDEA

The GROUPING idea is one of the basic features of well designed modern furniture. It is the idea which makes it possible to use the space in your rooms so that they are less crowded even though they provide more utilities.

The idea is simple. Let us take for example the average bedroom. Adequate equipment for a bedroom to be shared by two people requires TWO chests of drawers and a dressing table. These three pieces, together with the bed, require **four separate** walls in the case of old-fashioned furniture. However, very few bedrooms contain four wall spaces of such size and location as to permit the placing of four pieces so that they look well and are in the proper place in the room for convenient use.

The difference of one wall solves this problem. Almost all bedrooms do have three good wall spaces. If, therefore, we can get all the required pieces into the room by using only three walls, we can arrange a room properly.

In the case of the bedroom this is simple. Instead of having two chests of drawers of different sizes and shape, we use **two identical** chests which can be grouped, that is placed together, so as to form one unit, which occupies one wall instead of two.

And in addition, you achieve an entirely new **decorative** effect. One large group of chests gives a decorative center to the room which scattered units never achieve.

Following are diagrams of "before and after" which show how advantage is gained.

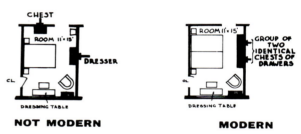

NOT MODERN **MODERN**

An even greater advantage is secured in the case of the living room; especially in the case of the **double purpose** room, the living-dining room, and the one-room apartment.

In a living-dining room of small size it is not possible to have desk space, book space, and dinette chest in the room in **good arrangement** when old-fashioned furniture is used. With modern furniture, however, it becomes simple, and an extremely interesting decorative effect is obtained with the long group of chests.

This is illustrated in the diagrams below:

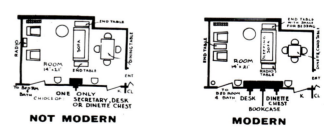

NOT MODERN **MODERN**

A one-room apartment which combines living, dining, and sleeping needs demonstrates the advantages of modern furniture to the fullest extent. One of typical size and shape is shown below. The modern arrangement **does everything** — all utilities are provided, free floor space remains at the maximum, and the decorative effect is strong and unified. For pieces for such a room see pages 4 to 39.

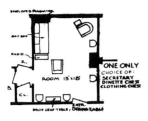

NOT MODERN

MODERN

POINTERS

The House — In order to use modern furniture it is not necessary to have a home designed in the modern style. Modern furniture fits into the apartment house and the majority of small houses. An apartment house is of necessity "modern" and to use 17th and 18th Century furniture and an electric elevator is simply an anachronism that continues because it hasn't been noticed.

Most single family houses do not possess any true historical characteristics and are modern in the sense that they are nothing else. Modern furniture is, therefore, at least as appropriate in these homes as any other type and in most cases more so.

The Room — Twentieth Century Modern furniture does not require any architectural setting other than plain flat walls, free from paneling or any other characteristic that is reminiscent of a historical style. Such plain walls are precisely the kind that are found in the majority of homes.

Painting of Walls — The architecture of the room must be considered for the distribution of colors on the walls; a wall with a fireplace, or one containing several doors, or an unbroken wall that is planned as the background for the largest group of furniture should be used as the deciding factor and the rest of the colors apportioned accordingly. A recessed portion of a wall, or an alcove often give an excellent basis for division of color.

In the case of bedrooms, wall paper should be selected not only with reference to the wood color of the furniture, but also to the spirit of the design — simple designs require simple patterns.

Window Treatment — Venetian Blinds or glass curtains are suggested in most modern rooms. It is not well to use both in one room and we recommend that only one or the other be used.

Over-curtains can be used when desired, in either plain, striped or modern figured fabrics. The important thing to remember is that the colors used must harmonize with the rest of the color scheme.

Floors — We suggest a plain colored broadloom carpet as a safe base for all rooms. Scatter rugs can be used over the carpet when desired, providing the colors and designs are in keeping with the rest of the room.

Accessories — The accessory furnishings should be, as in the case of any other furniture, in the same spirit as the furniture, but remember to keep them simple.

Pictures are good if the pictures are good. Some of the better magazines now regularly reproduce drawings by good artists. These are perfect for the small pictures when framed in plain narrow wood

frames, which can be unfinished wood or bright lacquer, or framed in the adjustable "Braquette" frames.

One More Pointer — Furniture and accessories are not selected primarily for their individual beauty and novelty; but what is of importance is the appearance of the ensemble when completed. The furnished room as **a unit** is what counts.

COMBINATION UPHOLSTERY

Two different cover materials may be used on DEEP ARM CHAIRS. Combination upholstery is not recommended on small chairs.

Division of the Fabrics — A number of different ways of making the combination can be used, and the method necessary varies with the design of the chair, but the simplest and safest way is to:

> Use the LIGHTER shade on the ENTIRE ARMS (inside, top, front, and outside) and the ENTIRE BACK OF BACK and the DARKER shade of color on the INSIDE OF BACK, TOP OF SEAT, and FRONT OF SEAT.

GENERAL PRINCIPLES OF COMBINATION

A — Combinations of two shades of the same colors are always good and generally are to be preferred to combinations of two different colors.

B — Combinations of two different colors are usually undesirable, except that **white, grey** and **black** combine well with almost any color.

C — Combinations of a **solid color** fabric with a **pattern fabric** of the same or different shade of the same color are particularly good.

D — Combinations of a plain **flat color weave** with a fabric of pronounced texture, but same color, are good, but never combine a dainty dressy fabric such as satin or rayon rep with a rough heavy fabric.

E — Combinations of two different weaves of **pattern goods are** bad.

F — Combinations of one plain and one pattern material can be used, but in that case keep the dominant color of the patterned fabric the same color as that of the plain fabric. Use plain fabric on arms and patterned fabric on seat and inside back.

Stripes are usually best horizontal on the back and same direction on the seat.

Never combine two different patterned goods.

G — Combinations of **lacquered** and **soft** fabrics are good. Use lacquered goods on the **arms**, soft goods on the **seat and back.** Such combinations look good if made with lacquered and soft fabrics of the same color, but they can also be made with a difference in shade or color. Do not use lacquered fabrics on seats and backs which have a lot of flex as the coating of the fabric will crack.

H — WELTING — No blanket rule can cover all cases but it is usually best in the case of combination upholstery to make all welts the color of the **dark** cover material. In any event use only one color of welts throughout. Do not use lacquered fabric for welts, especially on seats and backs.

CHEST GROUPINGS

THE HERMAN MILLER FURNITURE COMPANY *Living - Dining Group*

No. 3448 Two Bookcases, each 48 in. long

A bookcase group measuring 8 ft. wide. Any number of these can be used **together**. The length of the group can be varied in 2-ft. units by using the 24-in. Utility Chest with Rest-On Shelf as shown in group No. 1.

No. 3426 Utility Chest   **No. 3425 Desk**   **No. 3448 Bookcase**
32 in.   32 in.   48 in.

Total width of group 9 ft. 4 in. The 32-in. wide Bookcase can be used in place of the 48-in. one for a narrower group, or for a longer, other bookcases can be added.

No. 3448 Bookcase   **No. 3437 24-in. Utility Chest**
48 in.   **with 24-in. No. 3435 Rest-On Shelf**
                        24 in.

A utility bookcase group 6 ft. wide.

No. 3425 Desk   **No. 3448 Bookcase**
32 in.   48 in.

Total width of group 6 ft. 8 in. The Utility Chest No. 3426 can be used in place of the desk without changing size or appearance of group.

No. 3425 Utility Bookcase   **No. 3425 Console Ra**
32 in.   24 in.

Total width of group 4 ft. 8 in.

No. 3432 Bookcase   **No. 3425 Utility Bookcase**
32 in.   32 in.

Total width of group 5 ft. 4 in. NOTE: The 48-in. Bookcase No. 3448 does NOT combine well with the Utility Bookcase No. 3425.

No. 3425 Console Radio   **No. 3448 Bookcase**
24 in.   48 in.

Total width of group 6 ft.

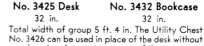

No. 3425 Desk   **No. 3432 Bookcase**
32 in.   32 in.

Total width of group 5 ft. 4 in. The Utility Chest No. 3426 can be used in place of the desk without changing size or appearance of the group.

No. 3432 Bookcase   **No. 3448 Bookcase**
32 in.   48 in.

A bookcase group measuring 6 ft. 8 in. overall. A 24-in. Utility Chest No. 3437, with 24-in. Rest-On Shelf can be added to make it 2 ft. wider.

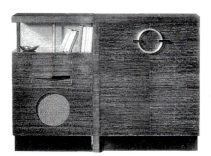

No. 2425 Console Radio   **No. 3426 Utility Chest**
(24-in.) with 24-in   32 in.
No. 3435 Rest-On Shelf

Total width of group is 4 ft. 8 in. The Desk No. 3425 can be used in place of the utility chest without changing size or appearance of the group.

No. 3426 Utility Chest   **No. 3425 Desk**
32 in.   32 in.

Total width of group 5 ft. 4 in.

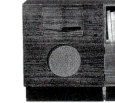

No. 3425 Desk   **No. 3435 Dinette-Utility Chest with**
32 in.   **48-in. No. 3436 Rest-On Shelf on it**

Total width of group 6 ft. 8 in. The 32-in. Utility Chest can be **used** in place of the desk without changing size or appearance of the group.

No. 3435 Dinette-Utility Chest   **No. 3425 Console Radio**
48 in.   24 in.

Total width of group 6 ft.

No. 3425 Console Radio   **No. 3437 24-in. Utility Che**
24 in.   24 in.

Total width of group 4 ft.

No. 3432 Bookcase 32 in.   No. 3425 Utility Bookcase 32 in.   No. 3435 Dinette-Utility Chest with 48-in. No. 3436 Rest-On Shelf on it 48 in.   No. 3425 Desk 32 in.

Total width of group 12 ft.

No. 3425 Utility Bookcase 32 in.   No. 3435 Dinette-Utility Chest with 48-in. No. 3436 Rest-On Shelf on it 48 in.

Total width of group 6 ft. 8 in.

No. 3432 Bookcase 32 in.   No. 3425 Utility Bookcase 32 in.   No. 3435 Dinette-Utility Chest with 48-in. No. 3436 Rest-On Shelf on it 48 in.

Total width of group 9 ft. 4 in. Any number of the 32-in. Bookcases can be added at the left.

No. 3437 24-in. Utility Chest 24 in.   No. 3435 Dinette-Utility Chest 48 in.   No. 3425 Console Radio 24 in.

Total width of group 8 ft.

No. 3432 Bookcases 32 in.

Total width of group 8 ft. Any number can be used together.

HEIGHT

There are only two heights of chest, the low, 30 in., and the high, 41 in.

Since there are only two heights the height can be readily seen on these photographs and is therefore not indicated under each group.

DEPTH

All chests are one depth, front to back, 15 in. This includes bookcases.

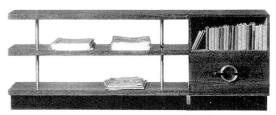

No. 3454 Open Bookshelves 54 in.   No. 3437 Utility Chest 24 in.

Total width of group 6 ft. 6 in. Combinations using the Open Bookshelves are especially well suited for use against the backs of sofas or the Ensemble Chairs No. 3457. They are of course also suited for use against a wall. The Console Radio No. 3425 also fits alongside these open bookshelves.

These Sheets Show Only a Few of the Possible Groupings

ALL the chests and bookcases in the Herman Miller Furniture Company Living-Dining group can be used in combination.

This combination use has important decorative and utilitarian value.

When grouped the cases have the appearance of a single piece of furniture, and because these groups can be arranged to fit whatever wall spaces there are in the room a "planned" or architectural "built-in" effect can be obtained which cannot be obtained with single pieces.

This grouping makes possible the efficient use of room space. Any size wall can be fitted with any utility without sacrificing decorative values.

THE HERMAN MILLER FURNITURE COMPANY, ZEELAND, MICHIGAN

WALL UNITS IN EAST INDIA LAUREL

The standard finish is natural, a grayish Walnut color — All cases 41 in. high

No. 3425 Desk
Open
L 32   D 15   H 41

The lower part of the No. 3425 Desk serves a number of utilities.
The right has shelves. Lower Deep Drawer for Vertical File.

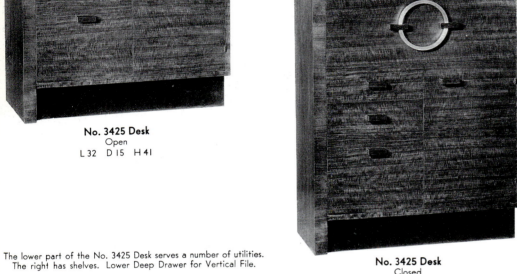

No. 3425 Desk
Closed
L 32   D 15   H 41

No. 3425 Bookcase
Closed
L 32   D 15   H 41

No. 3450 Chair
No. 3465 Chair
No. 3425 Desk
No. 3448 Bookcase
No. 3436 Rest-on Shelf
No. 3437 Utility Cabinet

WALL UNITS IN EAST INDIA LAUREL

Units 41 in. high

No. 3426 Utility Chest
Closed
L 32 D 15 H 41

No. 3426 Utility Chest
Open
L 32 D 15 H 41

No. 3635 Chest of Drawers
L 32 D 15 H 41

No. 3432 Bookcase
L 32 D 15 H 41

No. 3448 Bookcase
L 48 D 15 H 41

The No. 3426 Utility Chest is suited for clothing, table linen, silver and glasses, and is especially useful in the dining-living room or in the one-room apartment. The cork-lined trays are removable. One of the compartments just accommodates a portable typewriter.

All the pieces on pages 6 and 7 are of the same height and same depth and therefore are made to line up with each other on a wall. Any number of combinations can be made with three or four cases thus giving the furniture and also the room flexibility.

No. 3432 Bookcase
No. 3425 Wall Desk
No. 3425 Arm Chair

WALL UNITS IN EAST INDIA LAUREL

All units below are 30 in. high

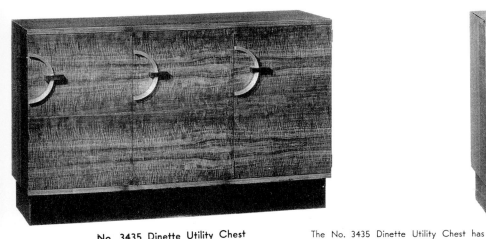

No. 3435 Dinette Utility Chest
Closed
L 48   D 15   H 30

The No. 3435 Dinette Utility Chest has three compartments, one with a shelf for tall utensils such as percolators; one fitted with tray drawers, the two upper ones lined with velvet for silver, the two lower for table linens; one fitted with cork-lined trays for glasses of various sizes. The trays are removable for serving. This chest is useful in various rooms.

No. 3435 Dinette Utility Chest
Open
L 48   D 15   H 30

No. 3454 Book Shelves
L 54   D 15   H 30

No. 3425 Console Radio
W 24   D 15   H 30

No. 3437 Utility Chest
L 24   D 15   H 30

No. 3436 Rest-on Shelf
L 48   D 15   H 11

The Rest-on Shelves are used in building up the 24- and 48-in. cabinets to get more height and space.

No. 3435 Rest-on Shelf
L 24   D 15   H 11

See pages 4 and 5 for chest groupings using Rest-on Shelf to obtain height.

EAST INDIA LAUREL

The Nos. 3632, 3633, and 3634 Bookcases, shown in the interior at the right in that order, are made as an individual group and do not line up with the other Laurel Bookcases. The two end Bookcases can also be used to make up a wall group and any of them can be used singly.

They are 32 in. wide, 11 in. deep, and 39 in. high.

LAUREL LIVING - DINING TABLES
EAST INDIA LAUREL

No. 3435 Console Dining Table
Closed
L 56   D 16   H 28

No. 3435 Console Dining Table
Open
L 56   D 32   H 28

No. 3568 Extension Table
Open
Laurel
T 30 x 60

No. 3568 Extension Table
Closed
Laurel
T 30 x 30

SUGGESTED PIECES FOR A ONE-ROOM APARTMENT

Incorporating living, dining and sleeping utilities in one room

EAST INDIA LAUREL

No. 3635 Chest of Drawers
L 32   D 15   H 41

No. 3580 Sleeping Sofa
Overall 36 x 78   Depth 33 without pillows
22 with pillows
Between Arms 74
12½ yards 50" material

No. 3580 Sofa (Open)

No. 3425 Day Bed End
L 46   D 15   H 24

These pieces are illustrated only to show how a one-room apartment can be furnished. For other wall units see pages 6, 7, and 8. For occasional and coffee tables see pages 12 and 13.

The No. 3580 Sofa has a lever which levels the seat. Then when the pillows are removed it forms an emergency sleeping unit for one person.

No. 3440 Box Spring Frame
Inside Measurement for Spring 74 x 33

No. 3441 Box Spring Frame
Inside Measurement for Spring 74 x 39

Interior below shows the No. 3440 Box Spring Frame fitted with a standard box spring and mattress covered with suitable upholstery fabrics to serve day time use as a sofa, and night time as a bed.

No. 3426 Utility Chest
Closed
L 32   D 15   H 41

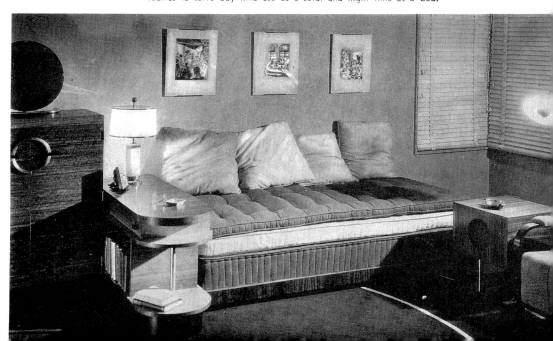

LAUREL OCCASIONAL PIECES
EAST INDIA LAUREL

No. 3548 Desk
Closed
T 44 x 22   H 29

No. 3548 Desk
Open with Portable Typewriter
The Pull-out is at the proper height for typing. The drawers are planned for convenient and orderly filing. The two lower trays can be removed to make storage space for the typewriter.

No. 3427 Flat Top Desk
L 44   D 19   H 29
Glass Top Only

No. 3436 Console
No. 3451 Chairs

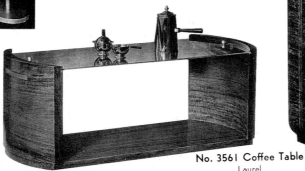

No. 3560 Occasional Table
T 40 x 18   H 16

No. 3561 Coffee Table
Laurel
B 17 x 42   H 16½

No. 3436 Console Table
L 42   D 12   H 27
Chrome Tubes

LAUREL OCCASIONAL PIECES
EAST INDIA LAUREL

No. 3551 Coffee Table
T 30 x 14   H 16

No. 3428 Coffee Table
L 32   D 14   H 18

No. 3552 Coffee Table
T 24 x 24   H 16

No. 3562 Occasional Table
Laurel
B 32 Dia.   H 16½

No. 3550 Occasional Table
T 24¾ Dia.   H 19

No. 3554 Occasional Table
T 18 x 18   H 16

No. 3549 Sofa End Table
T 30 x 13   H 20½

No. 3431 Sofa End Table
L 14   D 33   H 19

No. 3426 Chairside Table
L 12   D 15½   H 19

No. 3461 Sofa End Table
L 33   D 15   H 20½

No. 3460 Sofa Radio
W 33   D 15   H 20½

No. 3434 Radio Table
L 17   D 17   H 21

No. 3549A Lamp Table
T 30 x 13   H 20½

No. 3460 Table
No. 3461 Radio
No. 3457 Chairs

No. 7010 Drop Leaf Table
Top Closed 36 x 13
Top Open 66⅜ x 36
H 29
Can also serve as a desk with one leaf open.

No. 7012 Table
Top Closed 33 x 33
Top Open 33 x 66

No. 7014T Flat Top Desk
B 48 x 24   H 29

MAHOGANY DINING ROOM
ALL MAHOGANY

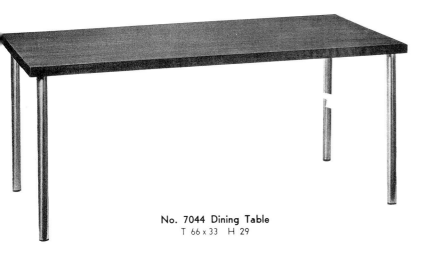

No. 7044 Dining Table
T 66 x 33 H 29

No. 7042M Buffet
L 60 D 17 H 37
With 9-in. wood supports call it No. 7042W.
With 5-in. wood supports call it No. 7142W.
No. 7042W Buffet same as No. 7042M but with metal
supports.
No. 7042 Buffet groups with No. 7003 Desk,
No. 7004 Chest of Drawers, No. 7005 Dinette
Utility Chest.
No. 7142 Buffet groups with No. 7104 Chest of
Drawers, No. 7105 Dinette Utility Chest.

No. 7043M China
W 36 D 13 H 49
With wood supports it is called No. 7043W.

No. 7018W Server
T 36 x 13 H 29
With metal supports it is called No. 7018M.

No. 7075 Dining Table
Dia. 48 H 29

No. 7045 Console and Dining Table
T 33 x 24 H 29
No. 7044 and No. 7045 line up together
All Mahogany
Metal supports are chrome plated.

MAHOGANY OCCASIONAL PIECES
ALL MAHOGANY

No. 7026 Occasional Table
Dia. 32 H 18
Glass Top

No. 7028 Occasional Table
Dia. 32 H 18
Glass Top

No. 7027 Chairside Table
L 22 W 14 H 18

No. 7029 Occasional Table
L 33 W 18 H 18
Glass Top

No. 7023 Occasional Table
Dia. 34 H 16
Wood Top

No. 7021 Sofa End Table
L 32 W 15 H 19
Contains two cigarette drawers,
which pull out from front

No. 3741 Corner Table
L 32 W 32 H 21½
Mahogany or E. I. Laurel

No. 7025 Occasional Table
Dia. 32 H 18
Wood Top

No. 7061 Sofa Radio Table
L 32 W 16 H 19

No. 7062 Sofa End Table
L 32 W 16 H 19

No. 3740 Chair Grouping Table
L 32 W 29 H 19
Mahogany or E. I. Laurel

THE WALNUT LIVING - DINING GROUP

This group includes all pieces needed for:

LIVING ROOM

COMBINATION LIVING-DINING ROOM

ONE-ROOM APARTMENTS

DINETTES AND BREAKFAST ROOMS

CONVENTIONAL DINING ROOM

LIBRARY OR DEN

PROFESSIONAL OFFICE

THE CHESTS and BOOKCASES in the group are developed on the **grouping principle** first introduced for American use by Gilbert Rohde in 1932, and represent the last and final development resulting from years of experience with this type of furniture, so that they provide the maximum of usefulness and flexibility together with fine lines and proportions. These units are planned in several sizes for various purposes as explained below.

All chests of the same height and depth can be grouped in a straight line. All chests of equal height can be grouped around a corner, even though depth of chests on wall is different from depth of chests on the adjoining wall.

WOODS — Wood is American Walnut Veneer, with some solid Walnut parts on outside surfaces. Inside of open compartments are also veneered with Walnut.

The chest group and the flat top desk have fine line inlays of White Holly.

One series of small occasional tables have solid White Maple legs as noted.

Drawer interiors are White Oak.

FINISHES — A choice of two finishes is available; **Natural** and **Dark.** The **Natural** finish gives the true color of unfinished Walnut, a light grey-brown, entirely free from the usual yellowish color imparted by finishing materials, yet is accomplished without any unnatural bleaching of the wood. This is a unique achievement in finishing. It is called Miller Grey Walnut.

The open compartments of chests and cases will always come finished "Dark" when the "Natural" finish is ordered. The interiors of these compartments are almost entirely hidden when books or other objects are in place, and the Dark finish here gives a better effect.

The **Dark Finish** is a conventional dark stained walnut, inside of open compartments being the same as the outside.

Small tables having Maple legs show special notation for finishes in the photographs.

THE CHESTS — Desk, Utility Chest, Deep Bookcase.

GROUPING — Can be used singly or any number can be grouped in any order desired. They can also be arranged on two adjoining walls so that they form a group that turns a corner. Corner fillers make this possible. If desired a group of these 16-in. deep chests can be used on one wall, joined to a bookcase (or group of bookcases) only 11 in. deep. The corner fillers take care of the difference in depth. Diagrams that follow explain this in detail. Width of these chests — 40 in.

LEGS — All three of these chests are available in a choice of two types of legs.

Type "L" leg is unique in furniture design. It is made of a tube of **Lucite** or clear transparent plastic with a delicate satin finish brass cap at the lower end. The transparent leg gives an effect of lightness as the furniture seems to be suspended in air. Leg "L" is 5 in. high, resulting in a finished chest height of 39 in.

Type "S" leg is of wood, also 5 in. high. This is in the skid design, but is unique in that it tapers toward the bottom, giving a lighter effect than the usual skid.

Two of the chests, the bookcase and the utility chest, are available in a third type of base, solid wood, 2 in. high. This results in a finished chest height of 36 in. This base cannot be used on the desk as the level of the writing surface would then be too low. This base is Type "F."

PULLS — Drawer and door pulls are of **Plexiglas,** another crystal-clear transparent plastic, that becomes almost invisible and gives beautiful unbroken wood surfaces on the fronts of the cases, catching only jewel-like reflections of light.

Three Shallow Drawers.

No. 3970-L Chest Desk
W 40 D 16 H 39
Closed

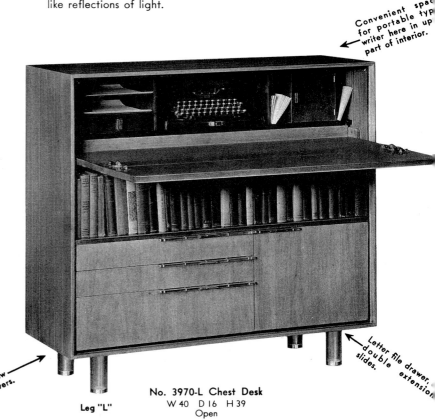

Convenient space for portable typewriter here in up part of interior.

Letter file drawer, double extension slides.

Leg "L"

No. 3970-L Chest Desk
W 40 D 16 H 39
Open

ALL WALNUT

No. 3942 Table
No. 3958 Chair

No. 3972L Utility Chest
No. 3971L Bookcase
No. 3970L Wall Desk
No. 90 Corner Filler

No. 3956 Chair

No. 3972-L Utility Chest
W 40   D 16   H 39

THIS CHEST can be used for glassware or general storage in living rooms, as buffet or dinette chest in combination living-dining rooms, as chest of drawers in a bedroom, or for storage of both dining equipment and clothing in a one-room apartment.

No. 3971-L Bookcase
W 40   D 16   H 39

No. 3950 Chair
No. 3974 Bookcase
No. 3975 Cabinet

No. 3975-F Low Cabinet
W 36   D 11   H 24
2 Doors with Adjustable Shelf Inside

No. 3974-F Low Bookcase
W 36   D 11   H 24

Either of the cases shown above can also be placed on top of either of the deep chests or desks. This can be done, however, only if the lower piece is used singly, as the low chest and bookcase are not the same width as the high deep chests.

CORNER GROUPING

All chests of the **same height** can be grouped around a corner regardless of the depth of the chests by the use of the Corner Filler. The Filler is attached to one case by metal plates screwed to the back. Diagrams showing how they can be used are shown below.

No. 90 Filler to be attached to Nos. 3970, 3971, 3972 Cases.
T 16 x 16   H 34

No. 91 Filler to be attached to Nos. 3970, 3971, 3972, 3973 Cases.
T 10¾ x 16   H 34

No. 92 Filler to be attached to No. 3973 Case
T 10¾ x 10¾   H 34

No. 93 Filler to be attached to Nos. 3974, 3975 Cases.
T 10¾ x 10¾   H 22

No. 3976 Bookshelves
W 54   D 15   H 28

ALL WALNUT

No. 3977 Desk
W 48   D 24   H 29

The No. 3977 Desk shown above has two drawers in the right pedestal. The top drawer is a partitioned drawer and the bottom drawer is a large vertical file also partitioned. The left pedestal has a Pull-out at the proper height for typing. It also has three trays. Removal of the lower tray provides storage space for the typewriter.

No. 3973-S Bookcase
W 40   D 11   H 39

No. 90 Corner Filler
W 16   D 16   H 34

No. 3973 Bookcases
No: 3977 Desk
No. 3965 Chair

ALL WALNUT DINING ROOM

No. 3979 China
T 36 x 14   H 50
All Walnut

No. 3979 Table
L 66   W 32½   H 30
Closed

No. 3979 Table
L 98   W 32½   H 30
Open

No. 3966 Chair
W 20½ x 24½ x 32
1½ Yards
Specify Button or Channel back

No. 3967 Arm Chair
W 24½   D 24½   H 32
1½ Yards
Specify Button or Channel back

No. 3979 Buffet
T 60 x 18½   H 32
All Walnut

For other Dining Chairs see pages 39, 40, 41.

ALL WALNUT LIVING-DINING PIECES

No. 3978 Console Dining Table
Closed
L 54   D 20   H 29½

No. 3978 Console Dining Table
Open
L 54   D 40   H 28¼

No. 3998 Table
T 30 x 30 Closed
T 39½ x 30 Open
H 29

No. 3947 Lamp Table
L 32   W 15   H Lower Part 19
Upper Part 24
Hardware — Statuary Bronze

No. 3997 Drop Leaf Table
Closed
T 36 x 13   H 29

No. 3997 Drop Leaf Table
Open
T 67 x 36   H 29
Legs — Statuary Bronze   Pulls — Plexiglas

ALL WALNUT OCCASIONAL PIECES

The occasional tables are broadly divided into three groups, a light design group, a group in heavier design which includes a set of "sectional" or "grouping" occasional tables and a drop leaf occasional table, and lastly, the glass and Lucite tables, a magnificent luxury group.

Finishes of Heavier Group:
    Natural: Gray Walnut as on cases.
    Dark: Dark Walnut as on cases.

No. 3991 Sectional Table
T 18 x 18 H 19

No. 3990 Sectional Table
T 18 x 12 H 19

No. 3993 Sectional Rack
T 18 x 12 H 19

No. 3992 Sectional Table
T 18 x 18 H 19

Nos. 3992 and 3990 Tables Combined

Nos. 3992, 3992 Tables

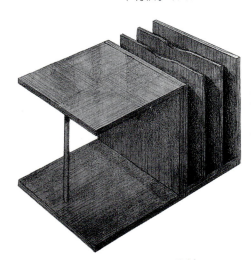

Nos. 3992 and 3993 Tables

Nos. 3992, 3990, 3992 Tables

Nos. 3991 and 3990 Tables Combined

Nos. 3991, 3990, 3991 Tables

The light group of occasional tables is comprised of the first four tables shown on this page, along with additional tables of the same design but different size. For these sizes see captions below cuts.

Finishes of Light Group:
    Natural: Top, Natural Walnut same as Gray Walnut shown on cases. Legs, light bleached Maple.
    Dark: Top and legs, stained Dark Walnut matching finish on cases when ordered "Dark."

No. 3984 Lamp Table
T Dia. 24 H 26

No. 3985 Occasional Table
T Dia. 30 H 17
2 hinged covers.

No. 3981 Occasional Table
T 44 x 22 H 15
No. 3980 Table (as above)
T 33 x 19 H 17
2 hinged covers.

No. 3996 Occasional Drop Leaf Table
T Open 48 x 16 H 18
T Closed 20 x 16 H 18
Legs: Statuary Bronze
Pulls: Plexiglas

The balance of the heavier group is shown below along with the No. 3996 Table above and also additional tables of the same design but different sizes.

No. 3982 Sofa End Table
T 30 x 15 H 22
Hinged covers at both ends.

No. 3949W Coffee Table
T 33 x 19 H 17

No. 3948W Coffee Table
T 40 x 20 H 16

No. 3995 Occasional Table
T Dia. 34 H 15
Wood Top
With 17 in. Height and 28 in. Dia. — No. 3940

No. 3994 Occasional Table
T Dia. 34 H 15
Glass Top
With 17 in. Height and 28 in. Dia. — No. 3941

No. 3949G Coffee Table
T 33 x 19 H 17

No. 3948G Coffee Table
T 40 x 20 H 16

No. 3944 Table   No. 3935 Sofa

LUXURY GROUP OF OCCASIONAL TABLES

These have a 3/4-in. thick plate glass top with polished edges. The legs are LUCITE tubes; Lucite is a sparkling, colorless, transparent plastic. The legs have satin finished brass caps at the lower end, and are attached to the glass top with heavy decorative machine turned brass fittings. This is a unique design by Gilbert Rohde of a luxury seen heretofore in custom designed pieces at many times the present prices.

The tables are shipped "knocked down," but the legs can be attached to the top without the use of tools.

No. 3942 Table
28 Dia.   H 17½

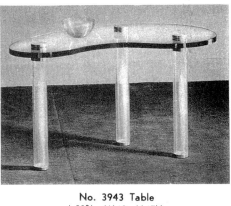

No. 3943 Table
L 29¾   W 18   H 17½

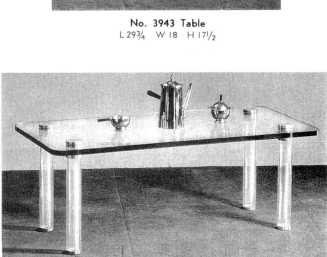

No. 3944 Table
W 44   D 22   H 15½

No. 3945 Table
D 34   H 15½

1 No. 3704 Double Sector Chair with 3 No. 3700 Straight Unit Chairs
1 No. 3550 Round Occasional Table
1 No. 3561 Coffee Table.
1 No. 3431 Sofa End Table

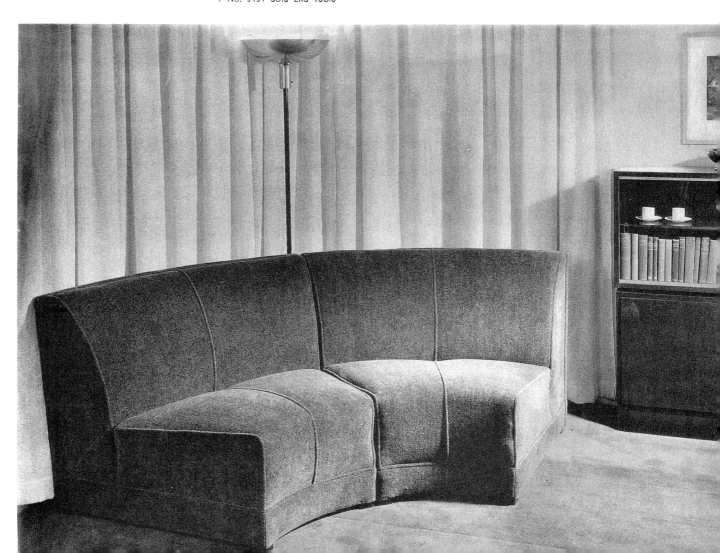

COMBINATION CHAIRS

No. 3700 Straight Unit Chair
Overall size 22 x 35½
H 30   Seat Height 16
3 Yards

No. 700 Arm
Overall size 32 x 14 x 3
1 Yard

No. 3701 Corner Chair
Overall size 35½ x 35½
H 30   Seat Height 16
5 Yards

No. 3704 Double Sector Chair
Overall size 92 x 35½
H 30   Seat Height 16
7¼ Yards
Curve of back on 60" Radius

No. 3708 Single Sector Chair
Overall size 46 x 35½
H 30   Seat Height 16
4⅓ Yards
Curve of back on 60" Radius

No. 3722 Two-Seater Sofa
Overall size 45 x 36
H 32   Seat Height 16
4½ Yards

No. 3703 is the Three-Seater matching above
Overall size 66 x 36
H 32   Seat Height 16
6 Yards

No. 3702 Round Corner Chair
Overall size 50 x 35½
H 30   Seat Height 16
5 Yards

For interior photographs showing these chairs see page 29.

COMBINATION CHAIRS

No. 3457 Flat Chair
22 x 31
Seat H 16   B H 32
2⅔ Yds. 50-in. Material

No. 3459 Corner Chair
31 x 31
Seat H 16   B H 32
4 Yds. 50-in. Material

*No. 258 Sofa Arm
1⅓ Yds. 50-in. Material

No. 257 is the two-seater sofa matching these chairs. Its length is 46 in.

*No. 357 Armless Sofa
L 68
7 Yds. 50-in. Material

* Use in combination with No. 3457 and No. 3459 Chairs.
Specify right or left (facing piece) when ordering Arm.

No. 3580 Sleeping Sofa
Overall size 36 x 78   Depth 33 without pillows
22 with pillows
Between Arms 74
$12\frac{1}{2}$ Yds. 50-in. Material

No. 3580 Sofa
Open

SOFAS

No. 3556 Sofa
With Welts
Overall size 80½   Between Arms 71½   D 22
16 Yds. 50-in. Material

No. 3546 Sofa
With Welts
Overall size 57   Between Arms 47   D 22
11 Yards 50-in. Material

No. 546 Sofa
Without Welts 10½ Yards

Fabrics with patterns or pronounced pattern in weaves, such as herringbone, not suitable for use on the outside of above pieces, if welts are desired. With such materials specify the number that calls for plain back.

No. 5272 Sofa
Birch
Overall size L 76   D 30
Between Arms L 66   D 22
11½ Yds. 50-in. Material

No. 3727 Sofa
Overall size 26 x 49
Seat H 18   H 33
Between Arms 46

EASY CHAIRS

No. 3555 Easy Chair
With Welts
Overall size 30 x 40
Between Arms 21   H 26
5½ yards 50" material

No. 3681 Square Back Easy Chair
Overall size 32½ x 45
Between Arms 22½ H 29¼
4¾ Yards

No. 3688 Barrel Back Easy Chair
Overall size 30 x 34½
Between Arms 22   H 31
5 Yards

No. 3687 Easy Chair
Overall size 29 x 41
Between Arms 23   H 29½
6 Yards

No. 3445-W Lounge Chair
Overall size 33 x 40
Between Arms 22   H 33
4½ yards 50" material

No. 3453-W Ottoman
Overall size 20 x 20   H 14
1½ yards 50" material

No. 3557 Easy Chair
Overall size 31 x 39
Between Arms 22   H 36
4½ Yards

No. 3425 Radio
No. 3681 Chair
No. 3549 Sofa End Table

EASY CHAIRS

No. 3454 Easy Chair
Overall size 31 x 30
Between Arms 21   H 29
3 yards 50" material

No. 3317 Chair
Overall size 29 x 33
Between Arms 22   H 31
3½ yards 50" material

No. 3685 Open Metal Arm Easy Chair
Overall size 28 x 33½
Between Arms 21   H 30
3⅓ Yards

No. 3451 Bentwood Chair
Overall size 24 x 29
Between Arms 22   H 27
2 yards 50" material

No. 3784 Round Back Easy Chair
Overall size 36 x 33
Between Arms 22   H 27
5 Yards

No. 3689 Easy Chair
Overall Size 26 x 34
Between Arms 22   H 30
2½ Yds. 50-in. Material

No. 3558 Round Back Chair
Overall size 27 x 34
Between Arms 21   H 31
3½ Yards

No. 7043 China
No. 3685 Chairs
No. 3740 Chair Grouping Table

No. 3705 Twin Grouping Chair
Overall size 26 x 32
Between Arms 22   H 27
3¹/₃ Yards

No. 3683 Round Back Chair
Overall size 28¹/₄ x 29¹/₂
Between Arms 22   H 27
3³/₄ Yards

No. 3682 Square Back Easy Chair
Overall size 28¹/₄ x 29¹/₂
Between Arms 22   H 27
4¹/₂ Yds. 50-in. Material

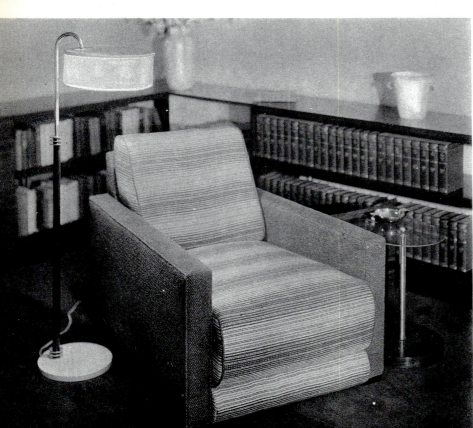

No. 3686 Pull-up Barrel Chair
Overall   size 26 x 28¹/₂
Between Arms 21   H 32
3¹/₄ Yards

DESK, BEDROOM AND DINING CHAIRS

Key for Modern Pull-up Chairs: A — Desk Chairs, B — Bedroom Chairs, D — Dining Chairs

No. 3425 Bentwood Pull-up Chair
W 23   D 24   H 32
1½ Yards
A — B

No. 3954 Bench
W 19   D 21¾   H 20
⅚ Yard
B

No. 3447 Arm Chair
W 25   D 28   H 33½
2½ Yards
A — B

No. 3968 Chair
W 23½   D 23   H 30
2 Yards
A — B

No. 3323 Ottoman
Dia. 18   H 17
1½ Yards
B

No. 3956 Chair
W 26   D 26   H 30
2 Yards
A — B

No. 3322 Arm Chair
W 22½   D 20½   H 31½
1⅓ Yards
A — B — D

No. 362 Ottoman
Dia. 21   H 18
2 Yards
B

No. 3322 Side Chair
W 20   D 20½   H 31½
1⅓ Yards
A — D

DESK, BEDROOM AND DINING CHAIRS

For key see page 39

No. 3725 Side Chair
W 20 D 24 H 33½
1⅓ Yards
A — D

No. 3726 Arm Chair
W 24 D 24 H 33½
1⅓ Yards
A — D

No. 5208 Side Chair
W 19½ D 19 H 31½
1 Yard
A — B — D

No. 3969 Arm Chair
W 23 D 22 H 31
¾ Yard
A — B — D

No. 3665 Chair
W 18 D 21 H 31
1 Yard
A — B — D

No. 5209 Arm Chair
W 23 D 19 H 31½
1 Yard
A — B — D

No. 3470 Chair
W 19 D 18 H 32
⅔ Yard
A — B — D

No. 3955 Bench
W 18½ D 25 H 19
⅔ Yard

No. 3957 Vanity Chair
W 19 D 24 H 25¼
1 Yard
B

No. 3471 Chair
W 19 D 18 H 32
1½ Yards
A — B — D

DESK, BEDROOM AND DINING CHAIRS

For key see page 39

No. 3960 Chair
W 20 D 22 H 31
⅚ Yard
A — B — D

No. 3961 Arm Chair
W 24 D 22 H 31
⅚ Yard
A — B — D

No. 3962 Chair
W 20 D 22 H 31
1⅓ Yards
A — B — D

No. 3963 Arm Chair
W 24 D 22 H 31
1⅓ Yards
A — B — D

No. 3965 Arm Chair
W 24 D 22 H 31
2 Yards
A — B

No. 3966 Chair
W 20½ D 24½ H 32
1½ Yards
A — D

Specify on order; buttons or channel back.

No. 3967 Arm Chair
W 24½ D 24½ H 32
1½ Yards
A — D

FORMAL DINING GROUP No. 3321
WALNUT WITH CHROME BASES

No. 5209 Arm Chair
W 23   D 19   H 31½
1 Yard

No. 3321 Oval Table
T 42 x 60   H 29
Extends to 96
3 apron fillers 42 x 12
Six Walnut Burl Inlays in Top
instead of two as shown.

For additional Dining Chairs see pages 39, 40, 41.

No. 5208 Side Chair
W 19½   D 19   H 31½
1 Yard

FORMAL DINING GROUP No. 3321
WALNUT WITH CHROME BASES

No. 3321 Buffet
T 66 x 17
Cork-lined Glassware Trays

No. 3321 Serving Cart
T 15 x 30
Also matches groups No. 3622 and No. 3725

No. 3322 Arm Chair
W 22½   D 20½   H 31½
1⅓ Yds. 50-in. Material

No. 3322 Side Chair
W 20   D 20½   H 31½
1⅓ Yds. 50-in. Material

No. 3321 China
T 14 x 36

FORMAL DINING GROUP No. 3622
WALNUT WITH BIRCH LEGS

No. 5209 Arm Chair
W 23   D 19   H 31½
1 Yard

No. 3622 Table
T 64 x 38   H 29
Extends to 96
3 apron fillers 38 x 10¾

No. 5208 Side Chair
W 19½   D 19   H 31½
1 Yard

For additional Dining Chairs see pages 39, 40, 41.

FORMAL DINING GROUP No. 3622
WALNUT WITH BIRCH LEGS

No. 3622 Buffet
Walnut
L 66   D 18½   H 33

No. 3622 Server
Walnut
L 32   D 17   H 30

No. 3960 Chair
W 20   D 22   H 31
5/6 Yd. 50-in. Material

No. 3961 Arm Chair
W 24   D 22   H 31
5/6 Yd. 50-in. Material

No. 3622 China
T 33½ x 16½   H 50

No. 3624
BEDROOM GROUP

WHITE ACER AND BLACK WALNUT

No. 3624 Dresser
No. 3625 Dresser
No. 3784 Chair

No. 3624 Left (facing) Dresser
Walnut and White Acer
B 43 x 18   H 36

No. 3625 Right (facing) Dresser
Walnut and White Acer
B 43 x 18   H 36

No. 3624 Bed
Walnut and White Acer
W 4 ft. 6 in. or 3 ft. 3 in.

No. 3624 Bedside Table
Walnut and White Acer
B 16 x 12½   H 27

No. 3624 BEDROOM GROUP

WHITE ACER AND BLACK WALNUT

No. 3624 Vanity
No. 3323 Ottoman

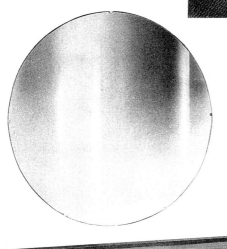

For bedroom Pull-up Chairs see pages 39, 40, 41.
For Easy Chairs for the bedroom see pages 35, 36, 37, 38.

No. 3624 Portable
16 x 16

No. 362 Ottoman
Dia. 21   H 18
2 Yards

No. 3624 Vanity
Walnut and White Acer
B 52 x 16   H 28   P 32 Dia.

No. 3624 Chest
Walnut and White Acer
B 32 x 18   H 44

NATURAL STRAIGHT
STRIPED WHITE ASH

No. 3317 Chair
Overall size 29 x 33
Between Arms 22   H 31
3½ Yards 50-in. Material

No. 3630 Dresser
Natural Straight Stripe White Ash
B 40 x 18   H 38
P 28 Dia.

No. 3630 BEDROOM GROUP
NATURAL STRAIGHT STRIPED WHITE ASH

No. 3968 Chair
W 23½ D 23 H 30
2 Yds. 50-in. Material

No. 3630 Vanity
Natural Straight Stripe White Ash
B 50 x 16 H 27
P 36 Dia.

No. 3323 Ottoman
Dia. 18
H 17

For bedroom Pull-up Chairs see pages 39, 40, 41.
For easy chairs for the bedroom see pages 35, 36, 37, 38.

No. 3630 Bedside Table
Natural Straight Stripe White Ash
B 14 x 11 H 24

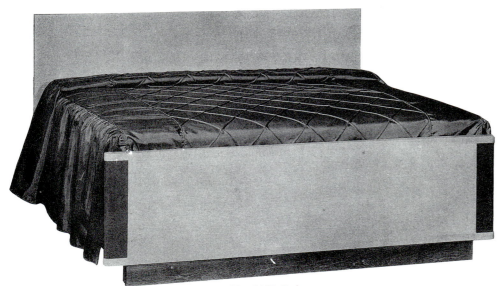

No. 3630 Bed
Natural Straight Stripe White Ash
4 ft. 6 in. and 3 ft. 3 in.

No. 3770
BEDROOM GROUP

BRAZILIAN ROSEWOOD
MAHOGANY INLAY

20 x 64 in. Mirror
No. 3770 Dresser Bases
No. 3784 Chair

No. 3454 Easy Chair
Overall size 31 x 30 H 29
3 Yards

No. 3770 Bedside Table
Brazilian Rosewood
T 14 x 16 H 27

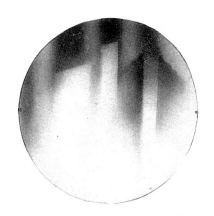

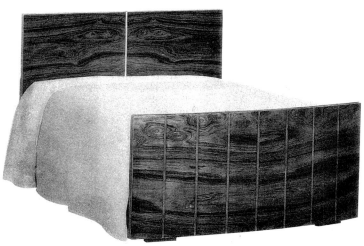

No. 3770 Bed
Brazilian Rosewood
4 ft. 6 in. or 3 ft. 3 in.

No. 3770 Dresser
T 46 x 19 H 34

No. 3770 BEDROOM GROUP

BRAZILIAN ROSEWOOD
MAHOGANY INLAY

No. 3770 Vanity
No. 3323 Ottoman

For bedroom Pull-up Chairs see pages 39, 40, 41.
For Easy Chairs for the bedroom see pages 35, 36, 37, 38.

No. 362 Ottoman
Dia. 21 H 18
2 Yards

No. 3770 Portable
Brazilian Rosewood
T 9 x 11¼
P 18 Dia.

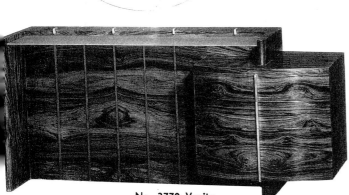

No. 3770 Vanity
T 56 x 18 H 26
Plain Round Mirror 36 in. diameter

No. 3770 Chest
Brazilian Rosewood
T 18 x 34 H 42

No. 3773 Dresser Bases
20 x 54 in. Mirror

No. 3773 Pe
T 11¼ x
P 18 Di

For bedroom Pull-up Chairs see pages 39, 40, 41.
For Easy Chairs for the bedroom see pages 35, 36, 37, 38.

No. 3773 Chest
Macassar Ebony and Quilted Maple
T 18 x 33   H 42

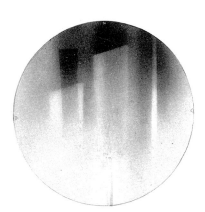

No. 3773 Dresser
Macassar Ebony and Quilted Maple
T 18 x 46   H 34
P 32 Dia.

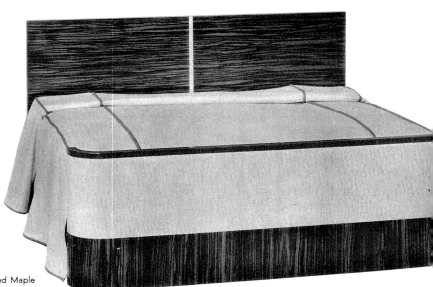

No. 3773 Bed
Macassar Ebony and Quilted Maple
4 ft. 6 in. or 3 ft. 3 in.

No. 3773
BEDROOM
GROUP

MACASSAR EBONY
AND QUILTED MAPLE

No. 3774 Dressing Table
No. 362 Ottoman

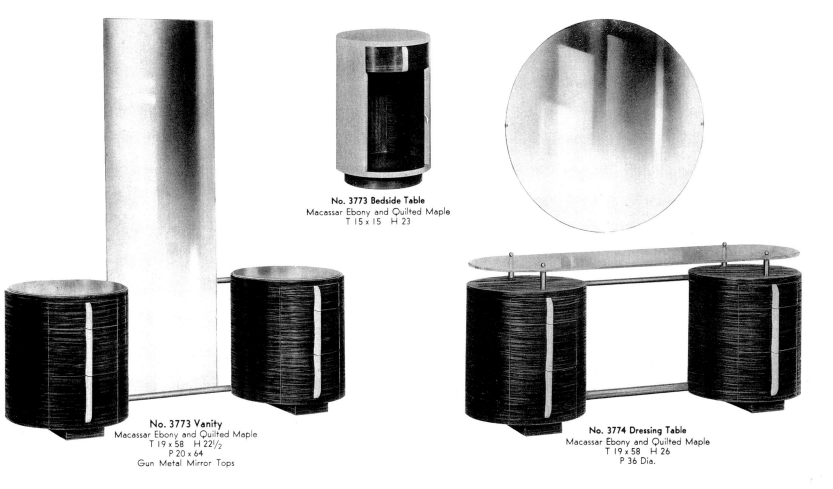

No. 3773 Bedside Table
Macassar Ebony and Quilted Maple
T 15 x 15   H 23

No. 3773 Vanity
Macassar Ebony and Quilted Maple
T 19 x 58   H 22½
P 20 x 64
Gun Metal Mirror Tops

No. 3774 Dressing Table
Macassar Ebony and Quilted Maple
T 19 x 58   H 26
P 36 Dia.

20 x 54 in. Mirror
No. 3930 Dresser Bases

For bedroom Pull-up Chairs see pages 39, 40, 41.
For Easy Chairs for the bedroom see pages 35, 36, 37, 38.

No. 3930 Bedside Table
T 11 x 15   H 26
Mahogany

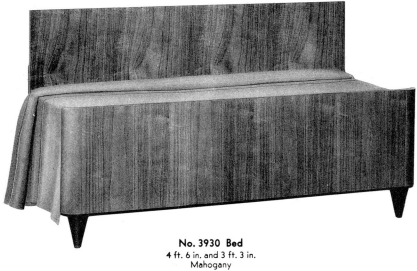

No. 3930 Bed
4 ft. 6 in. and 3 ft. 3 in.
Mahogany

No. 3930 Dresser Base
L 48   D 19   H 33
Dresser Mirror
33½ x 20

No. 3930 BEDROOM GROUP

ALL WALNUT
OR
ALL MAHOGANY

No. 3930 Vanity
No. 3955 Bench

Woods: Walnut with Bleached Maple Pulls.
Mahogany with either Bleached or Dark Pulls.
For Mahogany Finishes see page 15.

No. 3956 Chair
W 26   D 26   H 30
2 Yds. 50-in. Material

No. 3955 Bench
W 18½   D 25   H 19
⅔ Yd. 50-in. Material

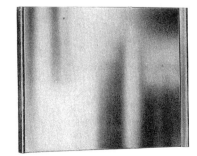

No. 3930 Chest
B 19 x 33   H 46
Mahogany

No. 3930 Vanity Base
L 48   D 18   H 27
Vanity Mirror
29½ x 24

No. 3910
BEDROOM GROUP

PALDAO AND QUILTED MAPLE

No. 3950 Chair
No. 3910 Dressers

For bedroom Pull-up Chairs see pages 39, 40, 41.
For Easy Chairs for the bedroom see pages 35, 36, 37, 38.

No. 3910 Bedside Table
D 14   W 16½   H 25

No. 3910 Dresser Base
W 48   D 18   H 33

No. 3910 Dresser Mirror
P 32 x 30

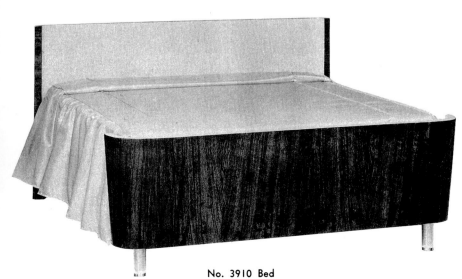

No. 3910 Bed
4 ft. 6 in. and 3 ft. 3 in
Headboard Height 33

The character of the following two bedroom groups is entirely different from Gilbert Rohde's previous work. His name has been associated with a rather severe but entirely functional style, but these groups are rich in decorative qualities and feeling of luxury. Mr. Rohde shows himself to be master of this style as he has been of functional design. Each of the suites combines many materials and uses both the curved and the straight line, but there is none of that confusion and disorganization of elements found so often when an attempt at luxury is made.

No. 3957 Vanity Chair
W 19 D 24 H 25¼
1 Yd. 50-in. Material

No. 3910 Vanity
No. 3957 Vanity Chair

In the No. 3910 group shown on these pages, the drawer fronts are slightly convex and covered in a newly perfected artificial leather in subtle tones of off-white and beige. The pulls for this suite are in the form of delicately thin strips of brushed brass.

The feature of this suite is the use of transparent legs. These are made of tubes of Lucite, which is a new colorless plastic. These legs have caps, also of brushed brass. A feeling of lightness, almost as if the pieces were suspended in air, is the effect obtained with this design.

No. 3910 Vanity Base
W 54 D 19½ H 27

No. 3910 Vanity Mirror
P 26 x 26

No. 3910 Chest
W 33 D 18 H 42½

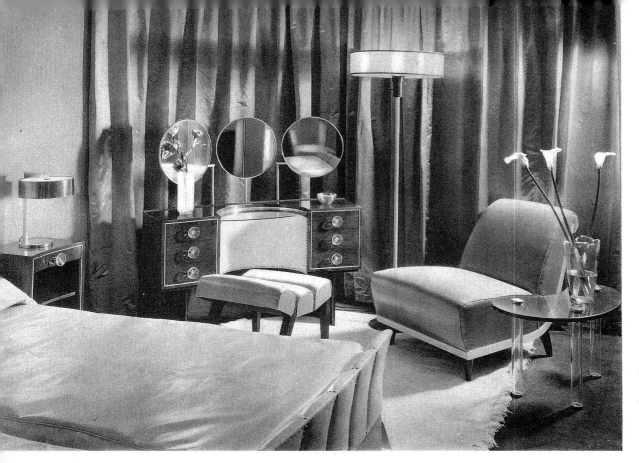

EAST INDIA ROSEWOO
AND
SEQUOIA BURL

No. 3920 Bed
No. 3920 Bedside Table
No. 3920 Vanity
No. 3951 Chair
No. 3943 Table
No. 3954 Bench

For bedroom Pull-up Chairs see pages 39, 40, 41.
For Easy Chairs for the bedroom see pages 35, 36, 37, 38.

No. 3920 Bedside Table
W 15 D 12 H 25

No. 3920 Dresser Table
W 46 D 19½ H 33

No. 3920 Dresser Mirror
P 32 Dia.

No. 3920 Bed
4 ft. 6 in. and 3 ft. 3 in.

61

In the No. 3920 group, Mr. Rohde emphasizes the use of Plexiglas for the pulls, combined with brushed brass decorative elements. The Plexiglas used for the pulls is a crystal-clear plastic that catches highlights with the brilliance of a diamond.

The same new off-white and beige artificial leather is used to cover the head and foot of the bed and also on portions of the cases.

The vanity in this suite as well as the No. 3910 is unique; this one in having adjustable circular triplex mirrors, framed in delicately thin brushed brass frames.

No. 3968 Chair
No. 3920 Dressers

No. 3920 Chest
W 34   D 19½   H 44¼

No. 3951 Easy Chair
W 29   D 37½   H 30
Seat Height 16
3 Yds. 50-in. Material

No. 3954 Bench
W 19   D 21¾   H 20
5/6 Yd. 50-in. Material

No. 3920 Vanity Base
W 50   D 16   H 28

No. 3920 Vanity Mirror
P 15 Dia.

TRADITIONAL GROUPS

THE Traditional line on the following pages has been planned to meet a real need. Time upon time the store or decorator is called upon to submit an ensemble of correlated pieces of authentic but uncommon design; matched in finish (sometimes in special finishes); of one high standard of quality; custom upholstered in harmonizing fabrics; not overpriced; preferably shipped at one time.

When such a need arises you will find it comparatively simple to plan your client's interior from these pages; and the selection and ordering from one source will greatly simplify your task.

The Traditional line is merchandized as "The Galleries of American Design," and divides into two types: 18th Century adaptations in living, dining and bedroom, and a smaller group inspired by the Shaker craftsmen of early American history (more about this on page 88).

Mahogany and Pine are used as harmonizing woods. Herman Miller Furniture Company has made pine furniture for a number of years. Pine pieces can be used altogether, or as complementing pieces with Mahogany. The two standard Mahogany finishes are Goddard and Museum. Goddard Mahogany is a hand-glazed, hand-padded finish, not distressed, and of substantial body. Museum is hand-distressed and hand-glazed, slightly lighter in color and body than Goddard. Both are block rubbed by hand.

The Pine finishes are Whittaker and Cambridge. Whittaker is a hand-treated finish not distressed, but giving the appearance of years of aging. Cambridge Pine is hand-distressed and antiqued to give the musty effect of a painted pine antique, washed off and restored.

Samples of the standard finishes sent on request. Special finishes can be matched for approximately 10% extra.

The same quality features in finish and upholstery and construction described on page 1 are found in the Traditional line.

LIVING ROOM

No. 735 Tuxedo Sofa
Overall size 74 x 30
Between Arms 65   H 32
Seat Height 19
9 Yards
Mahogany

No. 743 Open Arm Chair
Overall size 26 x 34
Between Arms 21   H 37
Seat Height 17   1¾ Yards
Mahogany

No. 756 Coffee Table
Top 32 x 17½   H 18
Pine

No. 6003 Table
L 13   W 13   H 31
Mahogany

No. 760 Coffee Table
T 32 x 16   H 21
Mahogany

No. 803 Breakfront Bookcase
W 64   D 17½   H 83
All Mahogany
Can also be used with 801 Dining Group on
pages 76, 77.

No. 742 Ladies' Club Chair
Overall size 31 x 30
Between Arms 21   H 36
Seat Height 19
5⅔ Yards
Mahogany

No. 3407 Desk
T 50 x 22   H 30
Pine
Leather Top

No. 604 Mirror
P 30 x 16
Pine

No. 600 Breakfront Bookcase
Base 56 x 22   H 80
Pine or Mahogany
Leather covered Writing Lid in
top upper drawer

No. 3487 Low Chest
Top 31 x 18   H 31
Pine or Mahogany
Leather covered Writing Lid

LIVING ROOM

No. 717 Desk
B 25 x 52½
H 30
Pine or Mahogany
Genuine Leather Top

No. 731 Barrel Chair
Overall size 33 x 27
Between Arms 21 H 37
Seat Height 17
4¾ Yards
Birch

No. 702 Arm Chair
W 24 D 23 H 36
1½ yards 50-in. material
Birch

No. 717 Desk
B 25 x 52½
H 30
Pine or Mahogany

No. 3488 Bookcase
T 36 x 12½   H 72
Pine Only
Plain Back

LIVING ROOM

No. 612 Desk
L 50   W 24   H 30
Genuine Leather Top
Mahogany and Birch

No. 700 Chair
W 19   D 19   H 32
1 Yard 50-in. Material
Birch
This chair with diamond tufted
Seat and Back is No. 777

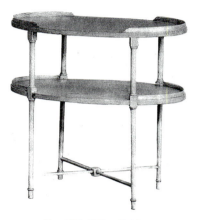

No. 750 2-Tier Table
L 27   W 18   H 27
Pine or All Mahogany

No. 709 Vanity Mirror
34 x 28
Pine

No.   746 Love Seat
No. 3403 Server
No. 3506 Chair

LIVING ROOM

No. 746 Duncan Phyfe Love Seat
Overall size 49 x 21
Between Arms 45½ H 34
Seat Height 17
2¼ Yards
Mahogany

No. 3403 Server
T 36 x 16½ H 34
Pine or Mahogany

No. 3506 Chair
W 20   D 19   H 37
⅔ Yard 50-in. Material
Birch

No. 755 Pembroke Table
L 37   W 17   H 29
All Mahogany

No. 901 Breakfront Bookcase
W 54   D 16   H 77
Mahogany

LIVING ROOM

No. 754 Living-Dining Table
L 54   W 23   H 31
All Mahogany

No. 737 Occasional Chair
Overall size 32 x 28
Between Arms 22   H 38
Seat Height 18
3²/₃ Yards
Mahogany

No. 751 Double Tier Table
L 30   W 17½   H 27
All Mahogany

No. 759 Bookshelf
W 29   D 10   H 37
All Mahogany

No. 747 Sofa
Overall size 74 x 34
Between Arms 65   H 34
Seat Height 18
10 Yards
Mahogany

No. 709 Dresser Mirror
30 x 24
Pine

LIVING ROOM

No. 3491 Bookcase
Size 54 x 14½ H 81
Mahogany and Birch
Desk Compartment in top drawer

No. 749 Barrel Chair
Overall size 31 x 24
Between Arms 22   H 35
Seat Height 19
2½ Yards Inside
1⅓ Yards Outside
Mahogany

No. 751 Table
No. 747 Sofa
No. 756 Coffee Table
No. 3506 Chair
No. 754 Table
No. 759 Bookshelf
No. 737 Chair

LIVING ROOM

No. 745 Hepplewhite Love Seat
Overall size 57 x 27
Between Arms 38   H 33
Seat Height 17
4½ Yards
Mahogany

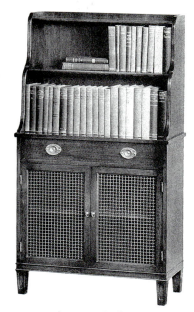

No. 907 Bookcase
W 25½   D 11½   H 47
Mahogany or Pine

No. 741 Occasional Chair
Channel Back
Overall size 32 x 28
Between Arms 21   H 38
Seat Height 18   4 Yards
Mahogany

No. 810 Desk
(Rear)

No. 810 Desk
L 49   D 25   H 30
Mahogany

No. 905 Table
T 15 x 18   H 27
Mahogany

LIVING ROOM

No. 808 Desk
L 46   D 23   H 30
Mahogany

No. 762 Book Rack
W 22   D 8   H 22
Pine

No. 761 Round 2 Tier Table
20 in. Diam.   H 26
Goddard Mahogany

No. 600 Bookcase
T 17 x 56   H 81
Lacquered on Pine
Raised Chinese Decoration in Black, Red or Yellow.
Leather covered Writing Lid on top of upper drawer.

FORMAL DINING ROOM
ALL MAHOGANY

No. 801 Buffet
L 68   D 22   H 36
All Mahogany

No. 802 Arm Chair
Overall size 23½ x 19   H 39½
Between Arms 20
⅔ Yard
All Mahogany

No. 801 Chair
Overall size 19½ x 17½   H 39½
⅔ Yard
All Mahogany

No. 801 Server
L 31   D 17   H 32
All Mahogany

No. 801 China
W 40   D 16   H 75½

No. 801 Table
Top Closed 66 x 44
Top Open 96 x 44
2 15-in. Fillers
All Mahogany

Also see No. 803 Breakfront, page 63, for a suitable piece with this group.

FORMAL DINING ROOM
ALL MAHOGANY

No. 803 Buffet
L 64   D 17½   H 35
All Mahogany

No. 802 Table
Top Closed 45 x 26
Top Open 45 x 68
H 30
All Mahogany

No. 803 Console Table
L 45   D 21   H 30
All Mahogany

No. 803 Breakfront on page 63 also matches this group

7

DINING ROOM
KNOTTY PINE
WHITTAKER OR CAMBRIDGE FINISHES

No. 702 Arm Chair
W 24   D 23   H 36
1½ Yds. 50-in. Material
Birch

No. 701 Refectory Table
T 54 x 36   H 30½
Extends to 90
Pine

No. 701 Secretary-China
B 16 x 37   H 74
Pine or Mahogany and Birch

No. 701 Side Chair
W 20½   D 23   H 36
1⅓ Yds. 50-in. Material
Birch

DINING ROOM
KNOTTY PINE
WHITTAKER OR CAMBRIDGE FINISHES

No. 701 Credenza Chest
B 18 x 54
H 36
Pine or Mahogany

No. 3507 Arm Chair
W 22½   D 20   H 37
¾ Yd. 50-in. Material
Birch

No. 3403 Server
T 36 x 16½   H 34
Pine or Mahogany

No. 3506 Chair
W 20   D 19   H 37
⅔ Yd. 50-in. Material
Birch

No. 707 BEDROOM GROUP
ALL MAHOGANY

8

No. 707 Chest
B 36 x 20 H 47
All Mahogany

No. 707 Bench
T 22 x 15½ H 22
Seat Height 18
½ Yard
All Mahogany

No. 707 Vanity
B 46 x 18 H 31
Mirror 31 x 22
All Mahogany

No. 707 Bed
Width 4 ft. 6 in. or 3 ft. 3 in.
All Mahogany

No. 707 Bedside Table
T 19 x 13 H 28
All Mahogany

No. 707 BEDROOM GROUP
ALL MAHOGANY

No. 707 Dressing Table
B 48 x 20   H 31
Mirror 31 x 22
All Mahogany

No. 707 Chair
W 15   D 17   H 33
Seat Height 18
½ Yard
All Mahogany

No. 707 Dresser
B 42 x 20   H 36
Mirror 31 x 22
All Mahogany

No. 709 BEDROOM GROUP

No. 709 Chair
W 16 D 18 H 33
Seat Height 18½
1¼ Yards
Birch finished Pine or Mahogany

No. 709 Chest
B 36 x 20 H 48
All Mahogany

No. 709 Dressing Table
B 48 x 18 H 31
Plate 32 x 22
Mirror Frame in Pine
Pine or Mahogany

No. 709 Bed
W 4 ft. 6 in. or 3 ft. 3 in.
All Mahogany

No. 709 Night Stand
T 17 x 13 H 27½
All Mahogany

No. 709 BEDROOM GROUP

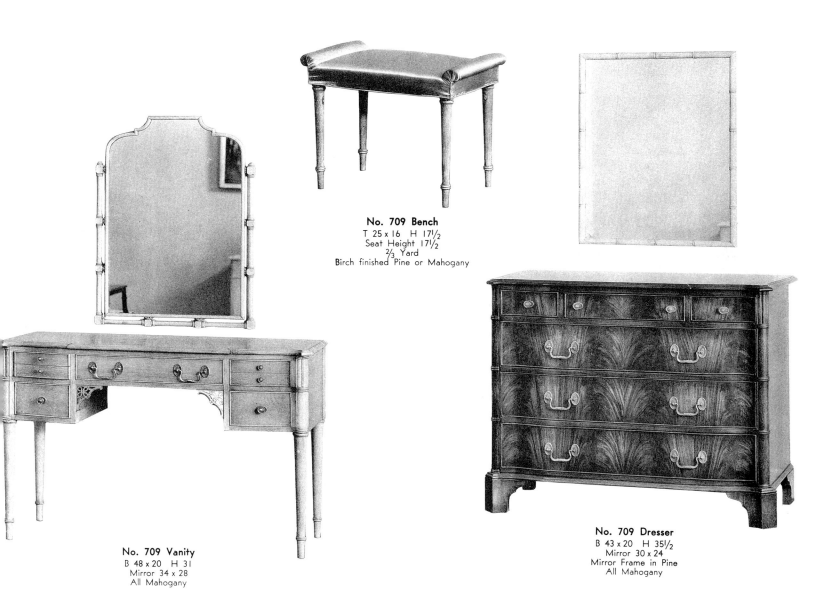

No. 709 Bench
T 25 x 16   H 17½
Seat Height 17½
⅔ Yard
Birch finished Pine or Mahogany

No. 709 Vanity
B 48 x 20   H 31
Mirror 34 x 28
All Mahogany

No. 709 Dresser
B 43 x 20   H 35½
Mirror 30 x 24
Mirror Frame in Pine
All Mahogany

No. 711 BEDROOM GROUP
ALL MAHOGANY

No. 711 Chest
B 38 x 21   H 50
All Mahogany

BEDSIDE TABLE,
MIRROR FRAMES AND
VANITY USUALLY
IN PINE

No. 711 Bedside Table
T 17 x 13   H 28
All Mahogany or Pine

No. 711 Bench
T 23 x 16   H 22
Seat Height 18
⅝ Yd. 50-in. Material
Birch finished Pine or Mahogany

No. 711 Bed
W 4 ft. 6 in. or 3 ft. 3 in.
All Mahogany

No. 738 Lounge Chair
Overall size 32 x 27
Between Arms 22   H 36
Seat Height 20
4⅔ Yards
Mahogany

No. 711 BEDROOM GROUP
ALL MAHOGANY

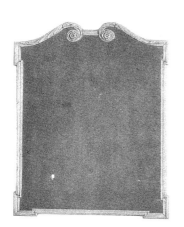

No. 711 Dresser
B 47 x 22   H 35
Mirror 33 x 24
Mirror Frame in Pine
All Mahogany

No. 711 Vanity
B 48 x 22   H 30
Mirror 28 x 23
Mirror Frame in Pine
All Mahogany or Pine

No. 711 Chair
Overall size 18 x 16   H 33
Seat Height 18
¾ Yd. 50-in. Material
Birch finished Mahogany or Pine

No. 712 Bed
W 4 ft. 6 in. or 3 ft. 3 in.
All Mahogany

No. 805 BEDROOM GROUP
ALL MAHOGANY
HOLLY INLAY

No. 805 Chair
Seat 18 x 17   H 17
Overall Height 32
1/2 Yard

No. 805 Chest
T 34 x 19   H 49

No. 805 Bed
Width 4 ft. 6 in. or 3 ft. 3 in.

No. 805 Bedside Table
T 16 1/2 x 14   H 27 1/2

No. 805 BEDROOM GROUP
ALL MAHOGANY
HOLLY INLAY

No. 805 Vanity Base
L 46   D 17   H 30
Vanity Mirror
28 x 34

No. 805 Bench
Seat 23 x 16   H 17
2/3 Yard

No. 805 Dresser Base
L 42   D 20   H 35½
Dresser Mirror
28 x 32

GALLERIES OF AMERICAN DESIGN

Shaker Wing

In planning "The Shaker Wing" of "The American Galleries of Design" the research work done by the Federal Art Project was of tremendous value.

The Shakers, as you probably know, were an American communal sect which first made its appearance in the New England States about 1790. Because of their radical beliefs, our Puritan forefathers would have nothing to do with them. By 1800 this isolation plus their religious beliefs began to tell in the characteristics of their craftsmanship.

The word "functional" had not yet come into being. The Shakers viewed sound construction and perfection of workmanship as indispensable evidence of man's willingness to labor faithfully according to God's ordinance. Beauty for its own sake was sinful. Thus they practiced functionalism that functioned in fact without benefit of elaborate theory; and at the same time from their religious preaching of simplicity, purity, and utility achieved beauty in pure form that was completely free from self-consciousness.

And so Herman Miller presents SHAKER FURNITURE — faithful expressions of the craft details and form ideals of the early Shaker pieces, which have a brightness and lightness of design expressive of serene and unworldly happiness.

No. 786 Shadow Box Mirror
P 34 x 26
Pine

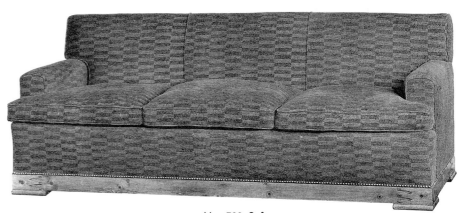

No. 729 Sofa
Overall size 80 x 34
Between Arms 69   H 33
Seat Height 18   10 Yards
Pine

No. 782 Circular Table
T 20 x 20   H 27½
Pine

SHAKER LIVING ROOM
KNOTTY PINE
WHITTAKER FINISH

No. 785 Living-Dining Table
Top Closed 60 x 20
Top Open 60 x 40
Height 30
Pine

No. 784 Flat Top Desk
B 50 x 22   H 30
Pine

No. 783 Coffee Table
T 27 x 27   H 18½
Leather Top
Pine

No. 727 Occasional Chair
Overall size 26 x 23
Between Arms 20   H 35
Seat Height 17
1½ Yards
Birch

No. 781 Lamp Table
T 29 x 17½   H 24
Pine

No. 763 Chair
Seat 18 x 15   H 33½
Seat Height 17½
Covered with webbing in either
Rust, Brown, or Natural Colors.
Birch

No. 780 Smoker Table
T 28 x 16   H 24
Pine

No. 728 Club Chair
Overall size 34 x 31
Between Arms 21   H 33
Seat Height 18
4½ Yards
Birch

No. 726 Open Arm Wing Chair
Overall size 28 x 27
Between Arms 24   H 38
Seat Height 17
4⅔ Yards
Birch

No. 730 Open Arm Chair
Overall size 25 x 24
Between Arms 19   H 37
Seat Height 17
3 Yards
Birch

SHAKER DINING ROOM
KNOTTY PINE
WHITTAKER FINISH

No. 723 Chair
W 17 D 18 H 33½
Seat Height 17½
½ Yard
Birch

No. 723 Extension Table
L 60 W 38 H 30
Extends to 8 ft.
Pine

No. 723 Corner Cupboard
W 28 D 15 H 71½
Pine

No. 724 Arm Chair
Overall size 21½ x 18½ H 35
Between Arms 17½
Seat Height 17½
½ Yard
Birch

No. 723 Server
T 30½ x 15 H 30½
Pine

SHAKER DINING ROOM
KNOTTY PINE
WHITTAKER FINISH

No. 764 Arm Chair
Size 18 x 15   H 33½
Seat Height 17½
Rust, Brown, or
Natural Webbing
Birch

No. 763 Chair
Birch
The cover shown
above is rust
webbing.
Size 18 x 15   H 33½
Seat Height 17½

No. 723 Welsh Cupboard
W 51   D 17   H 68½
Lower section usable as a
Buffet No. 723
Pine

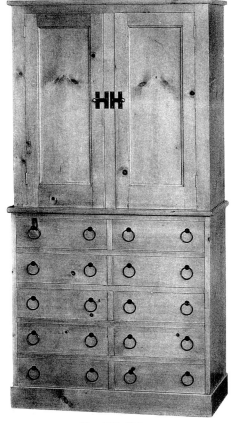

No. 723 China
W 30   D 15   H 62
Pine

No. 721
SHAKER BEDROOM GROUP
KNOTTY PINE
WHITTAKER FINISH

No. 721 Bedside Table
T 20 x 13   H 28

No. 721 Stool
Seat 14 x 14   H 25
Seat Height 16½

No. 722 Dressing Table
B 42 x 18   H 31
Mirror 18 x 13½

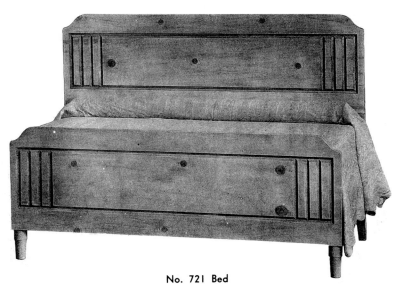

No. 721 Bed
4 ft. 6 in. or 3 ft. 3 in.

No. 721 Chest
B 36 x 20   H 52
Pine

Value Guide

Furniture is different from other decorative arts with regard to pricing, especially because condition ranges from the rare perfect piece to those showing degrees of wear and use. Furniture was used in someone's home or office — some pieces more lovingly than others — so prices will be affected by condition, including restoration. In addition, each region of the country will have a market directed by supply and demand, by individual tastes, and by fashions or trends. In the case of modern furniture, such as these examples by Gilbert Rohde for Herman Miller, the major coastal cities, plus other centers for modernism such as Chicago and Detroit, generally have the largest and most established markets, and perhaps the highest prices. Large European and Japanese cities have also shown keen interest in American modernism. Auctions often help to guide or set prices, but auctions are events, and once the lots are sold, similar examples at future sales may bring very different prices. Even though Rohde designs have already attracted the attention of many collectors and dealers, they are less well known than the classics by other Herman Miller designers, such as Charles and Ray Eames or George Nelson. Although Rohde was a prolific designer, his untimely death meant that his entire oeuvre spanned only about

ten years, and most designs were produced for only a few. There are no known records of the quantity produced for any of these Rohde designs.

With this in mind, it is clear that any price guide for modern furniture is apt to be uneven, to say the least, and *neither the author nor the publisher can be responsible for any outcomes from consulting this guide.* The only guarantee about this or any other value guide is that some readers will buy and/or sell outside of the listed range. That's a fact. Our intent is to give a general idea of some typical prices that similar items have recently sold for and might sell for again. It will also help to distinguish the relatively common from the highly desirable pieces. Prices are in United States dollars, and a range is given to account for different secondary market sources. It is assumed that pieces are in excellent condition with reasonable wear but no damage. Of course, the pristine example in near mint condition should command a higher price, and there is always the "sleeper" that is worth more than its price tag. Those are surprises that all collectors hope to find. In the meantime, I hope that this catalog brings you enjoyment and provides information that can improve the odds.

Chest Groupings		
pp. 4-5	open individual units	$400-600
	partially closed individual units	$600-800
	closed individual units	$500-700
Wall Units in East India Laurel		
p. 6	Desk	$600-900
pp. 6-7	Bookcases	$600-800
p. 7	Utility Chest	$700-900
p. 8	Dinette Utility Chest	$900-1,200
	Book Shelves, open	$400-600
	Console Radio	$400-500
	Utility Chest	$400-500
Laurel Living-Dining Tables		
p. 10	Console Table	$1,000-1,500
	Extension Table	$700-900
One-Room Apartment		
p. 11	Chests	$600-800
	Sleep Sofa	$800-1,000
	Bed End	$400-500
Laurel Occasional Pieces		
p. 12	Desk	$1,000-1,500
	Flat Top Desk	$1,200-1,800
	Console Table	$700-900
	3451 Chair	$900-1,200
p. 13	Occasional Tables	$400-800

Mahogany Wall Units		
p. 14	Desk	$800-1,000
	Bookcase, open	$700-900
	Bookcase, glass doors	$800-1,200
p. 15	Chest, Desk, Cabinet	$700-900
	7008W Bookcase, open	$500-700
	7008W Bookcase, glass doors	$700-1,000
	7109 Bookcase	$400-500
	7109 Bookcase, glass doors	$500-600
Mahogany Living-Dining Pieces		
p. 16	Drop Leaf Table	$1,200-1,800
	7012 Table	$600-800
Mahogany Dining Room		
p. 17	Table, rectangular	$600-800
	Table, round	700-900
	Buffet	$1,000-1,500
	China	$1,200-1,800
	Server	$400-600
Mahogany Occasional Pieces		
p. 18		$400-700
Walnut Living-Dining Group		
p. 21	Chest/Bookcase	$800-1,000
p. 22	Low Cabinet/Bookcase	$400-600
p. 23	Desk	$1,200-1,500

	Bookcase	$600-800
All Walnut Dining Room		
p. 24	China	$1,200-1,800
	Table	$1,200-1,500
	Chair	$300-400
	Buffet	$1,200-1,800
p. 25	Console Dining Table	$800-1,200
	Table	$400-600
	Lamp Table	$300-500
	Drop Leaf Table	$1,000-1,500
All Walnut Occasional Tables		
p. 26	top row	$200-300
	center row	$300-500
	bottom row	$500-700
p. 27	Occasional Tables	$500-900
Luxury Group Occasional Tables		
p. 28		$700-1,000
	3943	$800-1,200
p. 29	3704 Sections	$500-700 each
	Round Table	$800-1,000
	Coffee Table	$800-1,000
	End Table	$300-500
Combination Chairs		
p. 30	unit	$600-900 each
	Double Sector	$1,000-1,500

p. 31	Flat Chair	$600-800
	Corner Chair	$700-900
	Armless Sofa	$1,200-1,800
p. 32	Sleep Sofa	$800-1,200
p. 33	Sofas, 3-seat	$1,200-1,800
	Sofas, 2-seat	$800-1,200
p. 34	3935 Sofa	$1,500-2,000
	3706 Sofa	$1,200-1,500
	3666 Sofa	$1,400-1,800

Easy Chairs

p. 35		$600-800
	Ottoman	$200-300
p. 36	top row	$700-900
	center	$1,000-1,200
	Ottoman	$400-600
	bottom	$1,000-1,200
p. 37	Easy Chairs	600-800
	Bentwood Chair	$900-1,200
p. 38	Twin Grouping	$1,200-1,800
	Easy Chairs	$600-800

Desk, Bedroom, Dining Chairs

p. 39	Bentwood Pull-up	$500-700
	Bench	$300-400
	3447 Arm Chair	$500-700
	Chairs	$300-400
	Ottomans	$150-250
p. 40	top row	$300-400
	center row	$300-500
	bottom row	$300-400
	Vanity Chair	$400-600
	Bench	$300-400
p. 41	Side Chairs	$300-400
	Arm Chairs	$400-500

Formal Dining Group 3725

p. 42	Chair	$300-500
	Table	$1,200-1,500
p. 43	Buffet	$1,800-2,200
	Chair	$400-500
	China	$2,000-2,500

| | Server | $1,000-1,200 |

Walnut with Chrome Base

p. 44	Oval Table	$1,500-1,800
	Chairs	$300-400
p. 45	Buffet	$1,500-2,000
	Serving Cart	$400-600
	Chair	$300-400
	China	$1,800-2,200

Walnut with Birch Legs

p. 46	Table	$1,000-1,200
	Chair	$300-400
p. 47	Buffet	$1,000-1,500
	Server	$400-600
	Chair	$250-350
	China	$1,200-1,500

No. 3624 Bedroom Group

p. 48	Dresser	$700-900
	Chair	$600-800
	Bed	$800-1,000
	Bedside Table	$500-600
p. 49	Vanity	$1,200-1,500
	Ottoman	$300-400
	Chest	$1,000-1,200

No. 3630 Bedroom Group

p. 50	Chair	$600-800
	Chest	$1,000-1,200
p. 51	Chair	$300-400
	Vanity	$700-900
	Bed	$800-1,000
	Bedside Table	$400-500

No. 3770 Bedroom Group

p. 52	Dresser Bases	$1,000-1,200 each
	3784 Chair	$700-900
	3454 Easy Chair	$600-800
	Bedside Table	$500-600
	Bed	$1,500-2,000
	Dresser	$2,000-2,500

p. 53	Vanity, mirror	$2,200-2,700
	Ottoman	$300-400
	Chest	$2,000-2,500

No. 3773 Bedroom Group

p. 54	Dresser Bases	$1,500-2,200 each
	Portable Mirror	$200-300
	Chest	$2,000-2,500-
	Bed	$2,300-2,800
p. 55	Dressing Table	$2,500-3,500
	Vanity	$2,500-3,500
	Ottoman	$400-500
	Bedside Table	$700-900

3930 Bedroom Group

p. 56	Dresser Bases	$1,000-1,500 each
	Bedside Table	$300-400
	Bed	$1,000-1,500
p. 57	Vanity	$1,200-1,700
	Bench	$300-400
	Chair	$300-400
	Chest	$1,200-1,500

No. 3910 Bedroom Group

p. 58	Chair	$600-800
	Dressers	$1,800-2,200 each
	Bedside Table	$600-800
	Dresser Mirror	$300-400
	Bed	$1,200-1,500
p. 59	Vanity Chair	$400-600
	Vanity	$2,500-3,000
	Chest	$2,000-2,500

No. 3920 Bedroom Group

p. 60	Bedside Table	$500-700
	Bed	$1,200-1,500
	Dresser	$1,200-1,800
	Mirror	$200-300
p. 61	Chest	$1,200-1,800
	Bench	$300-400
	Chair	$600-800
	Vanity & Mirrors	$2,500-3,500